Food:
Nutrition & Invention

Grades 4-6

Written by Margot Southall
Illustrated by S&S Learning Materials

ISBN 1-55035-379-9
Copyright 1996
Revised January 2006
All Rights Reserved * Printed in Canada

Published in the United States by:
On the Mark Press
3909 Witmer Road PMB 175
Niagara Falls, New York
14305
www.onthemarkpress.com

Published in Canada by:
S&S Learning Materials
15 Dairy Avenue
Napanee, Ontario
K7R 1M4
www.sslearning.com

Look For

Other Health & Safety Units

F O O D

Nutrition & Invention

Table of Contents

Teacher Input Suggestions

1. Have your students brainstorm vocabulary related to the topic of Food and Nutrition in the form of a semantic web. Record the words and phrases in related groupings and ask the students to suggest category headings. Suggestions for category headings include:

- Fruits
- Vegetables
- Grain Products
- Milk Products
- Meat and Their Alternatives
- Fats, Oils and Sweets
- Food that Grows on Trees
- Food that Grows on Plants
- Parts of a Fruit
- Parts of a Vegetable
- Places to Buy Food
- Places to Eat Food
- Breakfast Foods
- Snack Foods
- Drinks
- Herbs, Spices and Condiments
- How We Preserve Food
- Food from the Sea
- Cooking Terms and Equipment
- Ethnic Foods
- Pasta
- Food Expressions
- Food Careers

You may wish to brainstorm questions the students have about each of these topics and have pairs of students research the answers and present them to the class daily. These questions and answers make an excellent bulletin board display and may also be used in a riddle center or a trivia quiz at the end of the unit.

2. Read a good novel to the class that reflects the topic of Food and Nutrition such as 'Chocolate Fever' by Kimmel Smith or 'James and the Giant Peach' by Roald Dahl. Alternatively, you may wish to read an informative book such as Marilyn Burn's 'Good For Me! All About Food in 32 Bytes', which has interesting sections on the invention of different foods as well as healthy eating and facts about digestion. The book "David Suzuki Asks: Did You Know ... About Food and Feeding" by Laura Suzuki and the video by David Suzuki entitled "Where Our Food Comes From" (see List of Resources) are also excellent springboards to the discussion of Food and Nutrition.

3. The Information Cards and corresponding Reading Information Activities may be presented in overhead form and used for whole group comprehension lessons or as an independent reading activity.

4. Use the Student Booklet in whole group sessions to introduce the necessary concepts and extend theme vocabulary, and as a springboard to class discussions.

5. Display a copy of your country's Food Guide. Discuss the foods in each food group and the suggested number of servings appropriate to the age of your students.

6. Focus on student eating habits by having each student record in chart form the number of servings of each food group he or she is eating daily over the period of a school week. Have students use a check mark to record each serving. You will need to explain combination foods such as chilli and pizza that belong to more than one category. At the beginning of the next week challenge students to improve their intake of neglected food groups.

Example:

Foods	Day 1	Day 2	Day 3	Day 4	Day 5
Fruit					
Vegetables					
Milk, Yogurt and Cheese					

7. Plan a visit to a local supermarket. Divide students into groups with each group responsible for one of the main food groups or "Other Foods" that do not belong in any specific food group. Explain that these are often snack foods that are high in fat, sugar or oil, and may also be beverages, condiments, herbs or spices. Prepare and distribute questions for students to answer during the field trip. You may wish to challenge your students to research the country of origin as one of the questions about their assigned food group.

8. Extend your students' understanding of geography and global interdependence. Ask them to find foods that are grown or processed in other countries and to bring the wrappers and labels to class. Record this in a bulletin board display. Glue an outline of a world map onto a large sheet of blank paper. As each student shares his or her research with the class, pin a label on the map identifying the name of that country and pin the wrapper on the blank paper around the map. Use wool or thread to join the country to the corresponding food wrapper. This creates an attractive web effect. Give your bulletin board a title, such as "Where in the World Does Our Food Come From?"

9. Discuss the inequities of the distribution of food resources in the world and the problem of famine. Ask your students for their ideas regarding the cause of food shortages. You may wish to address such topics as drought, population distribution and the problem of exporting cash crops instead of growing food crops for domestic consumption (e.g. coffee). The World Food Day Association has excellent resources available on this topic.

10. Compare good snacks and poor snacks in a chart form. Have students suggest a list of good snack choices. Explain the concept of empty foods that do not give the body any of the nutrients it requires. These foods can be listed as poor snack choices.

11. Discuss the concept of a food chain with your students. Apply this concept to different habitats they have studied.

12. Create a chart of the different cereals made from wheat, corn, oats and rice.

13. Ask your students to use the iodine test on selected foods to see if they contain starch. Add a few drops of iodine to some water in a jar. If this turns a blue/black color, the food contains starch. Students may also usethe fat test by seeing if a specific food leaves a greasy spot on paper.

14. Explain the term *vegetarian* to your students and discuss possible reasons for people making this decision, as well as the nutritional value of alternatives to meat.

15. Discuss how some foods were introduced to North America from other countries; for example, tomatoes and potatoes from South America, wheat from Spain and Portugal.

16. Display different vitamin and mineral supplements available and discuss each of the required vitamins and minerals and their purpose. Herbal or homeopathic medicine may also be of interest to your students.

17. Give each student an outline of a 24 hour clock. Ask students to mark on the time when theyhave their meals and snacks. Discuss what is the shortest gap between main meals, what is the longest gap between meals and other patterns in their daily eating.

18. Enjoy some classroom cooking experiences with your students. Have students copy and reassemble a recipe cut into sentence strips before they begin, to ensure understanding of the steps involved. Discuss kitchen measurements and utensils. The *Anne of Green Gables Cookbook* by Kate Macdonald may be of interest to your students.

19. Ask your students to record the advertisements for food and drink that they see on television over one or two days. Have them list the food and any slogans or promises made in the advertisements and describe how each one appeals to the viewer/consumer. Create a chart of slogans used by advertisers and ask your students to explain what they mean or decide if they do have a meaning. This may be an appropriate time to discuss the healthy ideal weight for different ages and body builds in addition to diet foods and the nutritional problems associated with students dieting while their bodies are still growing.

20. Create a graph representing your students' favorite sandwiches including the name of the sandwich, filling and bread used.

Example:

Name	Filling	Bread

21. Have your students make sweet smelling pomanders. Each student will need a small orange, pot of cloves and length of ribbon. Ask students to:

- tie the ribbon around the orange (i.e., four lengths around it)

- push the cloves into the orange skin so that they just touch each other. If the orange skin is very tough, have students use a knitting needle first

- put it in a paper bag in a cool, dry place for two weeks

- give it to a friend as a present

FOOD
Nutrition & Invention

Overall Expectations

Knowledge:

Students will:
- recognize the main food groups outlined in their country's Food Guide and the nutritional value of each group
- understand the nutritional requirements appropriate to their age
- identify the careers associated with food production
- demonstrate awareness of the global nature of our food resources
- identify the contributing factors to food shortages in the world

Skills:

Students will be able to:
- classify foods according to the main food groups
- demonstrate mapping and research skills
- locate the geographical sources of common foods

Affective:

Students will:
- develop an apreciation of the creative aspect of food preparation
- enjoy food related literature experiences
- appreciate the environment and the resources available to humankind
- value the human effort involved in providing our food resource

List of Vocabulary

Fruits

apples, apricots, banana, blueberry, cantaloupe, cherry, cranberry, grapes, grapefruit, guava, kumquat, lemon, orange, papaya, peach, pear, pineapple, plum, strawberry, watermelon

Vegetables

asparagus, beans, beet, broccoli, cabbage, carrot, cauliflower, celery, corn, cucumber, garlic, lettuce, mushrooms, onions, peas, pepper, potato, pumpkin, radish, rhubarb, spinach, squash, sweet potato, swiss chard, tomato, turnip, yams, zucchini

FOOD
Nutrition & Invention

Grain Products

bagels, barley, bread, cereal, corn, muffins, oats, pasta, pita bread, rice, rye, wheat, millet, sorghum

Meat and Alternatives

bacon, beans (dried), beef, chicken, duck, eggs, fish, goose, ham, lamb, lentils, mutton, nuts, peas (e.g. chick peas), poultry, peanut butter, pork, tofu, turkey

Milk Products

cheese (hard and soft cheeses), milk, yogurt

Cooking Terms

add, bake, beat, blend, boil, broil, chop, cream, crush, cut, decorate, dice, drain, drop, fold, grate, grill, knead, mash, measure, mince, mix, mould, pour, roll, scoop, shake, shape, scrape, sieve, slice, spread, sprinkle, slit, stir, toss, trim, whisk

Kitchen Utensils

baking dish, beaters, bowl, chopping board, cookie sheet, cooling rack, fork, frypan, garlic crusher, grater, jug, knife, measuring cup, peeler, muffin pan, pie dish, rolling pin, saucepan, spatula, spoon, whisk, wooden spoon

Measurements

cup, dash, grams, knob, ounce, liter, milliliter, pinch, sprinkle, tablespoon, teaspoon

Food Expressions

butter someone up	in a jam	ham it up
cold as ice	in a pickle	sour grapes
cool as a cucumber	like two peas in a pod	hot diggety dog
that's corny	red herring	sweet as pie
fishy story	save someone's bacon	

List of Skills

Reading Information:

1. Synthesizing Information
2. Sequencing Information/Context Cues
3. Recognizing the Main Idea
4. Locating Information/Illustrating
5. Making Inferences
6. Context Clues/Creating a Menu
7. Research/Illustrating
8. Identifying Definitions/Research

Language Activities:

1. Run-On Recipe
2. Homonyms
3. Dietary Definitions
4. Antonyms
5. Nouns, Verbs, Adjectives
6. Adjectives

Thinking Skills:

1. Diner Slang
2. Riddles
3. Careers in Food
4. Grains in Breakfast Cereals
5. Advertisements
6. Exercises for a Couch Potato
7. Invent a Health Food

Research Activities:

1. Sugar Detective
2. Traditions
3. Identify Global Sources
4. Herbs
5. Introduced Foods
6. Inventions
7. Ethnic Foods

Creative Writing:

1. Alliteraton
2. Journal of an Explorer
3. Menu
4. Giant Story
5. Recipe Book
6. Illustrate a Poem
7. The "Hole" Story

Art:

1. Sketch a Plant
2. Pasta Bridge
3. Cartoon
4. Snack Collage
5. Fitness Poster

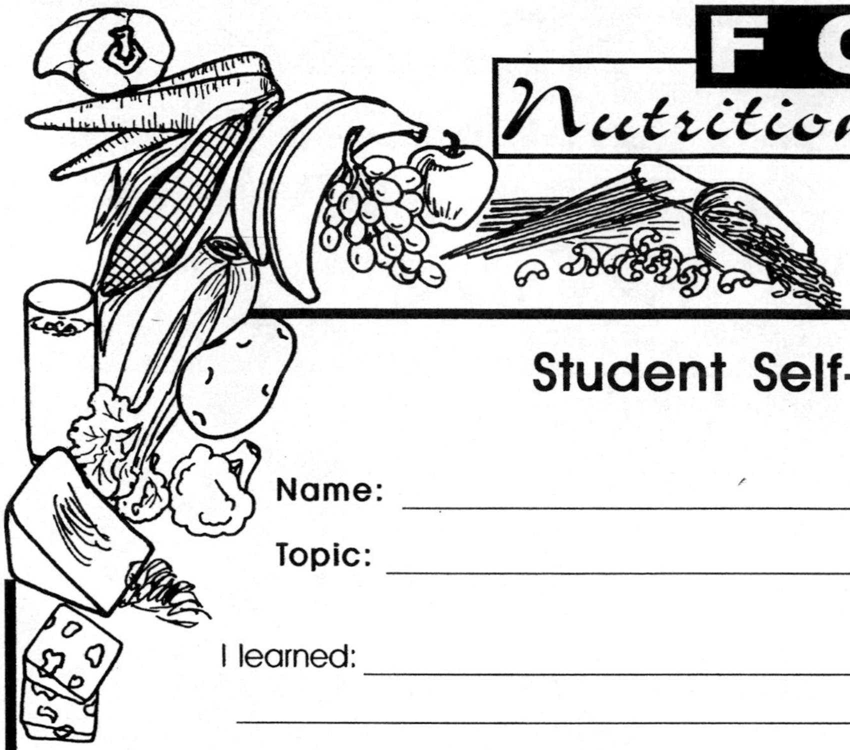

FOOD
Nutrition & Invention

Student Self-Evaluation

Name: _____   Date: _____

Topic: _____

I learned: _____

_____

_____

_____

I would like to know more about: _____

_____

_____

_____

My favorite activity was: _____

_____

_____

_____

My best work was: _____

_____

_____

_____

One area or skill I can imporve is: _____

_____

_____

_____

FOOD
Nutrition & Invention

Student Activity Tracking Sheet

Name: _____   Date: _____

Circle the number of each activity card that you have completed.

Reading Activity Cards

1   2   3   4   5   6   7   8

Language Activity Cards

1   2   3   4   5   6

Creative Writing Activity Cards

1   2   3   4   5   6   7

Research Activity Cards

1   2   3   4   5   6   7   8

Thinking Skills Activity Cards

1   2   3   4   5   6   7

Art Activity Cards

1   2   3   4   5   6

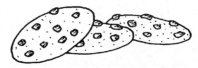

Fabulous Food!

Name: _____

Fabulous Food!

You Are What You Eat!

Food is more than something good to eat. Food gives us the energy to move and think. It is also the building material our body uses to repair itself and grow. Our body needs a number of different foods to do this. Look at a chart that summarizes the main food groups according to your country's Food Guide. How many food groups are there? We need to eat foods from each group every day to stay healthy.

Milk products include cheese, yogurt and other milk foods. These foods give us calcium for strong bones and teeth. Meat products and their alternatives include meat, poultry, fish, eggs, dried beans, and nuts. These foods are rich in protein. They are body building foods. They help us to grow. Grain products give us carbohydrates for energy. Vegetables and fruits are full of vitamins and minerals that protect us from sickness and keep us healthy.

How well did you eat yesterday? To find out, think about all the foods that you ate yesterday. Write them in the chart below. How many servings of each food group did you eat? Be sure to list the main food groups in your country's Food Guide in the left column.

Food Group	Foods	Number of Servings

Page One

Milk Products

cows	cream	taste	calcium
whey	processed cheese	rennet	pasteurized
gelatin	goats	germs	

In North America, most of the milk that we drink comes from _____. But in some countries people drink milk from other animals such as _____, sheep, horses or reindeer. Milk is made of water, milk, sugar, fat, protein, vitamins and minerals such as _____. The milk sold in the store has been heated quickly to kill any _____. It is called _____ milk.

Milk does not keep very long. We can keep the goodness of milk for a longer time by making it into cheese. Cheese is made from the milk of cows, goats and sheep. _____ is added to the milk to make cheese. This makes the milk separate into curds (solids) and _____ (liquid). The curds are used to make many different kinds of cheese. It takes about ten kilograms (22 pounds) of milk to make one kilogram (two pounds) of cheese. _____ _____ is made from heating up a mixture of ground up cheeses, whey powder, water and salt. Yogurt is made by adding a bacteria culture to heated milk. This mixture is kept warm for a few hours. The bacteria changes the _____ of the milk and thickens it. _____ can be added to make the yogurt set firmer.

Fabulous Food!

Meat and Alternatives

body building	fish	eggs	peanut butter
vegetarians	carp	shellfish	free range
fishing	beef	poultry	fish farms

Meat and their alternatives are _____ _____ foods. They are our main sources of protein. Meat also contains fats, vitamins and minerals. In countries where people eat very little meat, they may eat cereals, dried beans, lentils, peas and nuts for their protein. A person who chooses not to eat meat is called a _____. A vegetarian may get protein from those foods as well as milk and _____.

The most popular meats are _____ and veal (cattle), mutton and lamb (sheep), and _____ (chicken, turkey, ducks, geese). Other animals such as rabbits and goats are also raised for meat. We also eat _____ and _____ _____ for protein. Most of the eggs that we eat come from hens that are kept in cages on large battery farms. But some eggs are from _____ _____ hens. These hens can wander in the field during the day and return to their henhouse at night.

Many countries have large _____ industries. About 70 million tons of fish are caught every year. Fish contains protein, fat, minerals and vitamins. Fish can also be raised in _____. Trout and _____ are fresh water fish that can be kept in ponds. Some seafish are also raised along the coasts. _____ are a popular seafood. Crabs and lobsters are trapped in cages and shrimp are caught in nets.

OTM-406 • SSD1-06 Food: Nutrition & Invention

Grain Products

oat bran	seeds	cereals	wheat germ
flour	wheat	corn	breakfast cereal
rice	bran	cornmeal	carbohydrates

Grain products are made from the _____ of specific grasses. These seeds are called grains or _____. Grain products are the most important food to people all over the world. Wheat, rice, oats and corn are grains. Grains are also used to feed animals. Grains give us _____ and fats for energy as well as some protein. Cereals or grains are also an important source of the B vitamins.

More _____ is grown than any other cereal. It is the main ingredient in many of our foods. Most wheat is ground into _____. Wheat flour is good for making bread and pasta. Whole wheat flour is made by grinding the whole grain. To make white flour, the _____ and the _____ _____ are removed.

_____ is usually eaten as a whole grain instead of potatoes or in a salad. But rice can also be made into _____ _____, puddings, rice cakes and flour. When rice is cooked in water it will grow to three times its size. White rice is made by polishing the grains to remove the brown husk.

_____ can be eaten fresh on the cob, frozen or canned. Most of the corn the farmers grow is field corn. This is fed to animals or dried and ground to make _____. Cornmeal is used for muffins, cornbread and tortillas.

Oatmeal is made by drying the grains of oats and then flattening them with special machines. _____ _____ is the outer covering of oat seeds.

Vegetables

vitamins	potato	leaves	roots
sickness	energy	roots	fruits
potato	leaves		

Vegetables are necessary for good health. Vegetables give us _____ that help protect us against _____. They also give us carbohydrates for _____. You don't need to eat every vegetable to stay healthy, but you do need to eat a variety of different vegetables each day. The favorite vegetable in North America is the _____. Potatoes are full of goodness. They contain water, carbohydrates, protein, as well as minerals and a number of vitamins. A vegetable is any part of a non-woody plant that we eat.

Vegetables can be _____, flowers, seeds, stalks or stems, _____, tubers or bulbs. We usually think of tomatoes, cucumbers and beans as vegetables, but they are really _____.

Can you think of two vegetables for each category in the chart below?

leaves	flowers	seeds	stalks/ stems	roots	tubers/ bulbs

OTM-406 • SSD1-06 Food: Nutrition & Invention

Fabulous Food!

Fruit

bushes	citrus	tropical
pomes	vitamin C	berries
melon	drupes	trees

Many fruits are high in _____ _____. This vitamin helps protect us from sickness. There are six groups of fruits. _____ have a core and more than one seed.

Apples are pomes. _____ are fruits with a hard stone or pit. Cherries are drupes. _____ are fleshy fruits with many seeds. Strawberries are berries. _____ fruits such as oranges are pulpy.

_____ fruits grow in countries where the climate is very warm. We can see tropical fruits such as pineapples and bananas in our stores. Watermelons belong to the _____ family of fruits. Fruits grow on plants, _____, vines or _____. Strawberries grow on plants, blueberries grow on bushes, grapes grow on a vine and cherries grow on trees.

All fruits begin as a flower and every fruit has at least one seed. The seeds inside fruits can grow into new plants.

OTM-406 • SSD1-06 Food: Nutrition & Invention

Fabulous Food!

Can you think of **two** other fruits for each category below?

Pomes	Drupes
_____	_____
_____	_____
_____	_____
_____	_____

Berries	Citrus Fruits
_____	_____
_____	_____
_____	_____
_____	_____

Tropical Fruits	Melons
_____	_____
_____	_____
_____	_____
_____	_____

Page Seven

Fabulous Food!

The Food Chain

Every creature needs food to live. We get our food from the plants or animals that feed on plants. Plants can make their own food. Green plants use the sun's energy to make their food. Animals cannot make their own food. Many animals, such as mice, have to eat plants. Other animals, such as wolves, may feed on these plant-eating animals. This means that all animals and plants are linked together in a food chain.

Make a food chain.

Example:

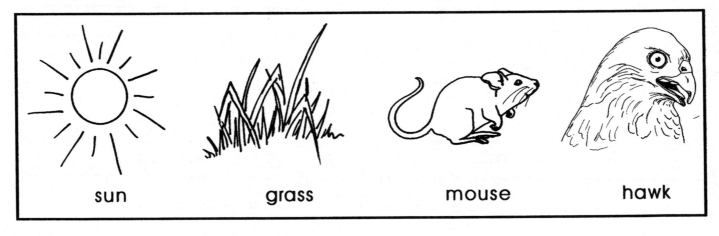

| sun | grass | mouse | hawk |

Energy and Plants   **Animals and Insects**

grass	corn	mouse	snake	mosquito
seaweed	lettuce	hawk	worm	chicken
wheat	sun	people	cat	wolf
oats	carrots	cow	frog	rabbit

Your Sense of Taste

tongue	salty	taste buds	bitter
sour	sweet	smell	digest
saliva	water	cold	throat

You taste your food with your _____. If you look in the mirror you will see little red bumps all over your tongue. These are your

_____ _____. You have four kinds of taste

buds. The taste buds at the tip of your tongue taste _____

foods. The ones at the sides of your tongue taste _____ things.

Further back on the sides are your taste buds for _____ foods.

The ones at the back of your tongue can taste _____

food.

Most foods are a mixture of these tastes. Your sense of _____

tells you a lot about how something tastes. Have you ever noticed that when

you have a _____ your food may not taste the same?

When you see food you like, your mouth may start to _____.

That is because your mouth is making _____ ready

for when you eat it.

Saliva or spit carries food over your taste buds and helps it slide down your

_____. Saliva also starts to _____ or

break down your own food.

Fabulous Food!

How many tasty foods do you know?

Make a list of sweet, salty, sour and bitter foods in the chart below

Sweet	Salt	Sour	Bitter

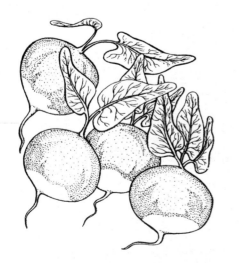

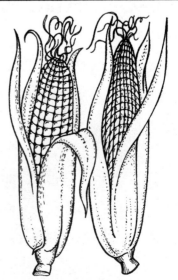

Page Ten

Fabulous Food!

Do You Have A Sweet Tooth?

fruit	honey	ketchup	breakfast cereals
sucrose	fructose	glucose	maltose
lactose	digest	energy	refined sugar

Sugar is added to many of the foods that we eat, such as _____ because it keeps them from going bad. If you read the list of ingredients on the labels of many processed foods you will see that there are different types of sugar. If you add up all the different sugars in some _____ _____ you will see that they contain more sugar than a candy bar!

There is _____. This is made from sugar cane or sugar beet. _____ is found naturally in fruit and honey. Vegetables and fruit contain _____. _____ is found in partly cooked cereals. _____ is the sugar in milk and dairy foods. Sugar gives your body energy, but too much can be bad for you health. The sugar we eat in cakes, cookies and candies is _____ _____.

Page Eleven

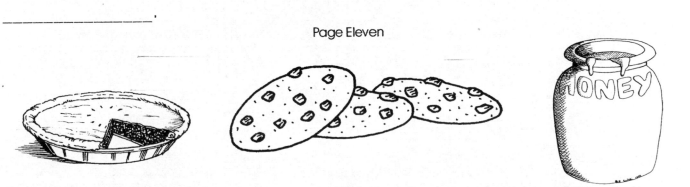

Fabulous Food!

Molasses contains a few vitamins and minerals, but refined sugar has no goodness left in it. The problem is that when sugar has been refined, our bodies cannot _____ it and it goes straight to our blood. This means that if you eat a candy bar you will quickly feel as if you have more _____, but it doesn't last long. It only takes a short time for our bodies to burn up the sugar and we are left tired and hungry again.

If you eat another food filled with sugar, your body will go up and then down again like a yoyo. This problem only happens when we eat sucrose in refined sugar. If we eat _____ or snacks with _____ our bodies will digest these sugars much better. This time we won't get a sugar "let-down". Instead, we will feel like we have more energy for a much longer time.

Page Twelve

Keeping Food Fresh

Food can go bad very quickly because tiny plants called bacteria grow on it if it is warm and moist. If the food is very cold, bacteria and moulds cannot grow on it. Refrigerators and freezers keep food fresh.

Another way is to dry the food. Bacteria and mould cannot grow without water. We eat dried foods such as raisins, and in some countries people dry fish and meat in the sun.

Make a chart.

Think of all the ways that we process vegetables and fruits, milk, fish, meat and cereals to keep them for a longer time. Make a list under each heading in the chart below.

Vegetables and Fruits	Milk
Fish	**Meat**

OTM-406 • SSD1-06 Food: Nutrition & Invention

Foods From Many Lands

Every country has its own special foods. A staple food is the most common food eaten in that country.

Match the menus to the right country. Print the name of the country and its staple food.

Countries	Staple Foods
Mexico	wheat bread
India	corn tortilla
Nigeria	chapatis and rice
Norway	yam and cassava

Menu One
tortillas with beans and chillies
corn, tomato and onion sauce
mangoes and melon

Country:_____

Staple Food:_____

Menu Two
pickled herring
salads and pickles
wheat bread
prunes and apricots

Country:_____

Staple Food:_____

Menu Three
beans and pepper stew
cassava dumplings
coconut pudding
banana

Country:_____

Staple Food:_____

Menu Four
bean and spinach curry
lentils, rice
chapatis
chutney, yogurt

Country:_____

Staple Food:_____

© On the Mark Press • S&S Learning Materials   OTM-406 • SSD1-06 Food: Nutrition & Invention

Fabulous Food!

In a Pickle!

We use food words in many of our sayings.

Example: | that's corny

Do we really mean what we say?

Think of a food saying that you know.

Print it and draw a picture of what it would look like if it really happened.

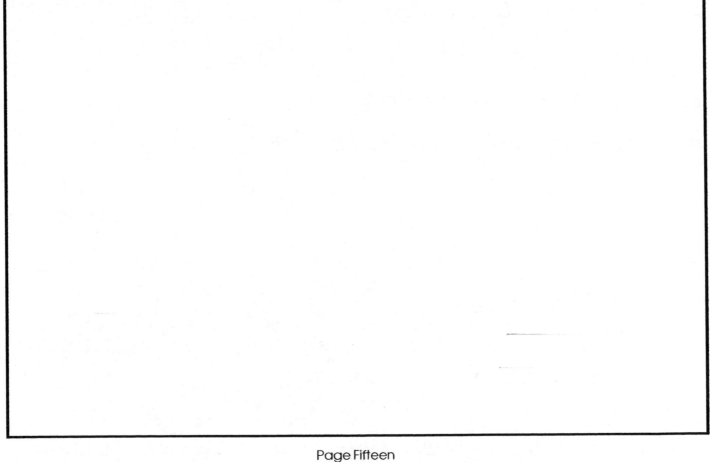

Fabulous Food!

Are You a Food Expert?

See how much you know about food.

Print **F** for **fact** and **O** for **opinion** next to each statement.

1. Some ice cream has seaweed in it. _____

2. Brown eggs are better for you. _____

3. If you eat just before bedtime you will have strange dreams. _____

4. Most of your body is water. _____

5. Chocolate will give you bad skin. _____

6. Broccoli is the most delicious vegetable. _____

7. An apple a day keeps the doctor away. _____

8. There are about 600 to 700 kernels on a cob of corn. _____

FOOD
Nutrition & Invention

Reading Information Card One

The Invention of Ice Cream

Once upon a time, kings and queens and rich people were the only ones who could enjoy ice cream. Long ago, an explorer named Marco Polo traveled all over China. When he returned home to Italy, he brought back recipes for frozen desserts named sherberts. Everyone loved them. When an Italian princess married the King of France, she brought the recipes with her. Everyone at the palace loved them and soon other kings and queens were enjoying the taste of ice cream. Some even tried to keep the recipe a secret, so only they could enjoy it.

Finally, one day the secret was shared and ice cream shops began to open. The first ice cream store in North America opened in New York City in 1774. But ice cream was still very expensive to make and most people could not afford to buy it. Then someone invented the home ice cream maker in 1846. You can still make ice cream by hand today, or you can use an electric ice cream maker.

Ice cream is made of cream, sugar, whole milk, milk solids, egg yolk or whole eggs, flavoring such as vanilla, and a stabilizer that stops ice crystals from forming. Vanilla is the most popular flavor, then chocolate and strawberry.

But how was the ice cream cone invented? Well, a waffle maker invented the ice cream cone in 1904. He was selling his waffles next to an ice cream stand. The ice cream seller had run out of dishes for his ice cream. So the waffle maker rolled one of his waffles into a cone shape, let it cool and filled it with ice cream. It was a hit!

Twenty years later, Americans were eating 245 million ice cream cones a year. There are now more than 400 different flavors of ice cream. Which is your favorite?

The Invention of Peanut Butter

The year 1990 was the one hundredth birthday of peanut butter. Peanut butter was invented in 1890 by a doctor in the United States. He was trying to find a food that had lots of protein and was easy to digest.

We need about 44 grams (1.5 ounces) of protein every day. Just one tablespoon of peanut butter will give you eight grams (0.3 ounces) of protein, as well as important vitamins and minerals.

How do you make peanut butter? It's simple. First you roast some Spanish peanuts, let them cool, take off the skins and then grind them up. Now you have the perfect peanut butter!

The peanut butter we buy in the store usually has salt and sugar added to it. You need to read the label to find out just what was added to the peanuts. All peanut butter must be at least 90 percent peanuts. That is the law.

Have you ever noticed that sometimes peanut butter separates into a solid lump covered with oil? This is nothing to worry about. You just need to stir it to have smooth peanut butter again.

What is your favorite kind of peanut butter? Do you like it chunky or smooth? Do you like it with sugar and salt added or just plain? How do you like to eat it? In a sandwich? How about peanut butter cookies? Ask your friends how they like their peanut butter.

Reading Information Card Three

The Invention of the Potato Chip

Today, potato chips are the biggest selling snack food in the United States and Canada. On average, we eat about 4.5 kilograms (10 pounds) of potato chips every year.

Potato chips were invented about 150 years ago, but it took a long time before you could buy them in a store. Like many inventions, the potato chip happened by accident.

In 1853, a chef named George Crumb worked at the Moon Lake Lodge in Saratoga Springs, New York. One night a customer complained about George's French fried potatoes. He said the potatoes were too thick and he sent them back to George in the kitchen. George cut the French fries thinner and sent them back, but the customer still didn't think that they were thin enough. So George sliced the potatoes as thin as a piece of paper and cooked them in hot oil. The customer loved them. They were thin, crisp and delicious. Everyone wanted to try them and George decided to call his invention "Saratoga Chips". The problem was they had to be made by hand and you could only buy them in restaurants.

In 1920, someone invented the potato peeling machine. Now factories could begin to make potato chips for everyone. A salesman named Herman Lay sold bags of potato chips all over the southern part of America. Lay's Potato Chips became the first American brand of this crunchy snack.

Reading Information Card Four

The Invention of Chewing Gum

The first pioneers in America learned to chew gum from the Native Peoples. This was not the chewing gum that we know today. The pioneers were chewing gum or resin from the black spruce tree.

In 1850, John Curtis decided to begin a chewing gum business using the gum from this type of tree. He cooked the gum until it was thick, rolled it out and cut it into small pieces. He and his son sold a lot of their "Pure Spruce Gum".

It was not until 1906 that the first bubble gum was invented. Frank Fleer called his bubble gum "Blibber-Blubber". The problem was that it was too sticky. When your bubble broke, you had a sticky mess all over your face. At last, in 1928 the "Dubble Bubble" was invented by Walter Diemer. His bubble gum was not so messy.

Today, if you travel to Japan you can find 150 different flavors of bubble gum. In the United States and Canada we also chew mountains of bubble gum. What is your favorite bubble gum?

Reading Information Card Five

The Invention of Pop

How did water, sugar and bubbles become popular? Well, it all started in 1767, when a scientist named Joseph Priestly found out how to make carbonated water. He was also the man who discovered oxygen.

The idea of bottling this fizzy drink began when Joseph moved to the United States. But it was not a successful business until 1832, when a man named John Matthews advertised his soda pop. Up to now, no one had thought to use advertising and we know that this makes a big difference. His soda pop sold well, even though it was just plain carbonated water.

It was still another 50 years before anyone added flavor to pop. In 1900, the favorite flavors were: root beer, ginger, lemon, cola, cherry, and sarsparilla.

Cola drinks are the most popular today. How do people make Coca-Cola and Pepsi? Well, the recipes are a secret. But if you read the list of ingredients on a can of Coke you will see that it contains carbonated water, sugar, caramel color, phosphoric acid, natural flavorings and caffeine. Caffeine is the same drug that is in coffee. It makes your heart beat faster and when you first drink it your body may feel like it is racing. Soon after, you may feel tired. This is because your body has used up the caffeine and there is no "real" food in pop for it to use for energy, only sugar and water.

So why do so many people drink pop? Well, the first reason is that it is advertised a great deal on the television and in magazines. The second reason is they like the taste. We each need to think about what we are feeding our bodies and make up our minds about what kind of pop we drink and how much we drink.

Reading Information Card Six

The Invention of Breakfast Cereal

Did you have cereal for breakfast this morning? There are so many cereals to choose from today. But who invented the first one? Maybe you will recognize this name. It was Dr. Kellogg. Dr. Kellogg was trying to find a food that was easy to digest for the sick people he looked after. He created a breakfast cereal made from flakes of corn. He called them "Kellogg's Toasted Corn Flakes". Today this is the most popular breakfast cereal in North America.

Breakfast cereals are big business. They are a quick and easy way of making breakfast. Many advertisements on television are made to sell different cereals. You can buy cereals in fancy shapes, chocolate or fruit flavored, and cereals with all kinds of things added to them.

Breakfast cereal began as a healthy food, but now many cereals have more sugar in them than cereal. Some even have more sugar in one serving than a candy bar. The only goodness is in the milk. It is important for us to read the list of ingredients on the box to see how much sugar there is in our cereal. If sugar is listed first, then there is more sugar than anything else in the box. Corn syrup, honey, molasses, sucrose, glucose, and fructose are all sugars. We need to be smart shoppers and check to see what is really inside our box of cereal.

Breakfast is the most important meal of the day. Our body has used up all the protein and energy foods that we ate the day before. There are many healthy cereals that will give our body the food it needs. Or, you could try something new for breakfast. A tub of yogurt, a peanut butter sandwich or a grilled cheese sandwich with a glass of juice or milk will give you the protein that you need to feel good all morning. Breakfast does not have to be boring. Just think of all the different foods that could start your day off right!

Reading Information Card Seven

Does Chocolate Grow On Trees?

The answer is: yes it does! The cacao (Kak-a-o) tree grows in South America and in West Africa. The pink flowers have green pods that are 15 to 25 centimeters (6 to 10 inches) long. They look a little like a small melon. When the pods are ripe the farmers cut them open and scoop out the beans. These beans are put into boxes or covered with leaves and left out in the hot sun for a few days to ferment. During this time they change from white to purple and then to a brown color. Next, they need to be dried for about ten to twenty days. Finally, they are cleaned and roasted. This brings out the chocolate flavor. Now they are ready to be shipped all over the world.

Some of the roasted beans will be made into cocoa powder and others will be made into chocolate. The beans are ground up and the cocoa butter is squeezed out to make cocao powder. This leaves a dry, brown cake which is crushed into powder. The cocoa butter that is left over is used to make chocolate. This is what gives chocolate its creamy, rich taste.

Unsweetened baking chocolate is made from whole ground beans. Sweet chocolate is formed by adding sugar, extra cocoa butter and flavoring to whole ground up beans. Milk chocolate is made by adding milk to sweet chocolate and then grinding the mixture until it is very fine and smooth. Milk chocolate contains carbohydrates, fats and protein, as well as vitamin A, calcium and iron. Carbohydrates are foods that give us energy. Mountain climbers and soldiers sometimes use chocolate to give them quick energy.

Chocolate does contain caffeine, but only a small amount. A can of cola has between 32 to 65 milligrams (0.0011 to 0.0023 ounces) of caffeine.

But who made the first cup of cocoa? Long ago the people in Mexico served a drink called "chocolatl" to the Spanish explorers. These explorers brought some cocoa beans home and the wonderful flavor of chocolate became one of the world's favorites. How many foods made with chocolate can you name?

Let's Look at Spices

Do you like spicy food? Did you know that ketchup and mustard have spices in them? We add spices to both sweet and savory food to give it flavor. Spices grow on plants and trees in tropical countries where it is warm all the time. Most of the spices we see in the store have been ground up into powder. But if you look at whole spices you can see what part of the plant they came from. Pepper grows on a tall vine. The pepper berries grow in bunches like grapes. Black peppercorns are berries that have been picked and dried. White peppercorns are ripe berries that have been soaked and had their husks taken off. Do you like black or white pepper on your food?

Have you ever eaten a gingerbread man? Ginger is made from a root that grows underground. When these roots have been dug up they are washed, scraped and left outside to dry.

Have you ever seen a cinnamon stick? Cinnamon is made from the bark of a tree. The sap in the cinnamon tree gives it its flavour. The workers cut pieces of bark from the branches, press them together and roll them into "quills". Then they are left to dry.

Nutmeg is made from a fruit that grows on an evergreen tree. When it is ripe it splits open and falls to the ground. The nutmegs are left to dry in their shell. When the nutmeg is loose enough to rattle, it is ready to be taken out of its shell. You can crack the shell open like a nut.

Cloves look like dried up flower petals. They are buds which are picked before they can open up into flowers. Mustard is made from the seeds of the mustard plant.

Spices are shipped all over the world so we can enjoy them thousands of kilometers (thousands of miles) from where they grow. Each spice has its own smell and taste. Some are mixed together. If you eat a pumpkin pie or Christmas cake you can taste the combination of cinnamon, nutmeg and cloves. A recipe for homemade ketchup might include pepper, ginger and cloves. Some spices give a hot flavor. These are pepper, chilli and ginger. Others such as cinnamon give a sweet flavor. Next time you are in the supermarket take time to look at the different whole spices there.

Reading Information Activity One

Read the Information Card called "The Invention of Ice Cream".

A) Print **true** or **false** after each sentence.

1. The first ice cream cone was made from a waffle. _____

2. Chocolate is the most popular flavor of ice cream. _____

3. The first ice cream store in America was in Orlando, Florida. _____

4. Long ago, only rich people could have ice cream. _____

B) Answer each of the following questions in complete sentences.

1. What is the most popular flavor of ice cream?

   _____

   _____

2. Where was the first ice cream store in America?

   _____

   _____

3. What invention made it possible for everyone to enjoy ice cream?

   _____

   _____

C) List **three** foods under each of the following flavors:

Vanilla	Chocolate	Strawberry

Reading Information Activity Two

Read the Information Card called "The Invention of Peanut Butter".

A) List **three** foods with peanut butter that you like to eat:

_____

_____

_____

B) List the **four** steps in making peanut butter:

1. _____   2. _____

3. _____   4. _____

C) Use words from the story to complete the sentences below.

1. The doctor who invented peanut butter was trying to find a food that

    had lots of _____ and was easy to _____.

2. Most peanut butter has _____ and _____

    in it.

3. Sometimes peanut butter separates into a _____,

    covered with _____.

Reading Information Activity Three

Read the Information Card called "The Invention of the Potato Chip".

A) List **three** other dishes made with potatoes.

1. _____
2. _____
3. _____

B) Answer each of the following questions in complete sentences.

1. Who invented the first potato chip?

   _____

   _____

2. Why did he cut the French fries so thin?

   _____

   _____

3. What did he call his invention?

   _____

   _____

4. Why couldn't you buy potato chips at the store before 1920?

   _____

   _____

5. Which new machine made it possible for factories to make potato chips?

   _____

   _____

Reading Information Activity Four

Read the Information Card called "The Invention of Chewing Gum".

A) Answer the following questions in complete sentences.

1. Who taught the first pioneers to chew gum?

_____

_____

2. What was the first chewing gum made of?

_____

_____

3. What was the problem with the "Blibber-Blubber" gum?

_____

_____

4. Which country has the most flavors of bubble gum?

_____

_____

B) Invent a new kind of bubble gum. Give it a name. What flavors will it come in? List the ingredients it is made with. Draw a picture of the wrapping paper with the name of the bubble gum.

Example:

Name: _____

Flavors: _____

_____

Ingredients: _____

_____

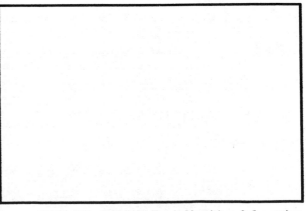

Reading Information Activity Five

Read the Information Card "The Invention of Pop".

A) List **two** advertising slogans that you have heard on television or the radio that advertise pop.

1. _____

2. _____

B) Describe the effect caffeine has on your body. Explain why this happens.

_____

_____

_____

_____

C) Think of **three** drinks that you could have instead of pop. List them below.

1. _____

2. _____

3. _____

Reading Information Activity Six

Read the Information Card called "The Invention of Breakfast Cereal".

A) Copy and complete the sentences below with the words from the Information Card.

1. Dr. Kellogg was trying to develop a food that was easy to _____.

2. The first breakfast cereal was called _____ _____ _____ _____.

3. Many _____ on television are made to sell cereal.

4. Now many breakfast cereals have more _____ in them than cereal.

5. Breakfast is the most important _____ of the day.

B) Create a breakfast menu for each day of the week that is both healthy and delicious.

Monday	Tuesday	Wednesday	Thursday	Friday	Saturday	Sunday

Reading Information Activity Seven

Read the Information Card called "Does Chocolate Grow On Trees?".

A) List **six** different foods that are made with chocolate.

1. _____
2. _____
3. _____
4. _____
5. _____
6. _____

B) Draw a picture of what you think a cacao tree looks like when:

- the pods are full of cocoa beans

- it is covered with pink flowers

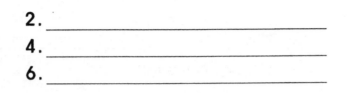

C) Think of a new kind of chocolate bar.

- What will you call it?

- What kind of filling will it have?

Draw a picture of your chocolate bar.

Print the name of your chocolate bar.

List the ingredients on the wrapper.

Reading Information Activity Eight

Read the Information Card called "Let's Look at Spices".

A) Spices come from different parts of plants and trees. Print the name of the spice that matches the descriptions below:

1. root _____

2. bud of a flower _____

3. bark of a tree _____

4. fruit that grows on a tree _____

5. vine _____

B) List **two** spices used in sweet dishes:

1. _____ **2.** _____

C) List **three** spices used in Christmas cake:

1. _____ **2.** _____

3. _____

D) List **two** spices that are used in hot dishes:

1. _____ **2.** _____

E) List **two** spices that are used in desserts.

1. _____ **2.** _____

Language Activity One

Run-On Recipe

A recipe is a short list of instructions.

Read the following recipe and correct the run-on sentences.

Copy each instruction and put a capital where a new sentence begins and a period where each sentence ends.

Lemon Meringue Pie

1. in a saucepan, mix sugar, cornstarch, flour and salt gradually add hot water, stirring constantly cook and stir over moderate heat till mixture comes to a boil reduce heat, cook and stir two minutes longer remove from heat

2. stir a moderate amount of hot mixture into egg yolks, then return to hot mixture bring mixture to boiling and cook two minutes, stirring constantly add butter and lemon peel slowly add lemon juice, mixing well

3. pour into pastry shell spread meringue over filling bake at 350⁰ F for twelve to fifteen minutes cool before cutting

Language Activity Two

Homonyms

Homonyms are words that sound the same, but have different meanings and spellings.

Example: **pair** - two of a sort
pear - a fruit

beet - beat	steak - stake
meat - meet	plain - plane
sauce - source	pear - pair
hole - whole	piece - peace

1. If this _____ is ripe, I will eat a _____ of them.

2. I would like to eat a _____ doughnut, not just a doughnut _____.

3. I will _____ you at the _____ counter in the supermarket.

4. If I give you a _____ of my chocolate bar, will you give me some _____ and quiet?

5. We could burn that old wooden _____ when we barbecue the _____.

6. I would like to learn the _____ of that mushroom _____ recipe.

7. All I could eat on the _____ was a _____ bagel.

8. The recipe said to _____ the salad dressing and then add the sliced _____.

Language Activity Three

Dietary Definitions

Research the following words in a dictionary.

Write the definition next to each word.

1. calorie: _____

   _____

2. energy: _____

   _____

3. vegetarian: _____

   _____

4. nutrient: _____

   _____

5. digestion: _____

   _____

6. famine: _____

   _____

7. protein: _____

   _____

8. fiber: _____

   _____

9. carbohydrate: _____

   _____

10. vitamin: _____

   _____

Language Activity Four

Antonyms

Antonyms are words that mean the opposite.

Example: hot - cold

Write the antonym next to each word below.

1. sweet _____

2. hot _____

3. messy _____

4. moist _____

5. empty _____

6. cooked _____

7. thawed _____

8. best _____

9. stale _____

10. big _____

Language Activity Five

Nouns, Verbs and Adjectives

A **noun** is the name of a person, place or thing.

A **verb** is an action word.

An **adjective** describes a noun. It tells more about the noun.

Choose a short poem about food.

List **four** nouns, verbs and adjectives that are used in the poem.

Example:

Nouns	Verbs	Adjectives

FOOD
Nutrition & Invention

Language Activity Six

Describe a Food

Adjectives are words that describe nouns. They tell more about them.

Think about each of the foods listed. How do they look, smell and taste?

Choose an adjective to describe each food and print it next to the food.

1. _____ chocolate cake

2. _____ steak

3. _____ apple pie

4. _____ salad

5. _____ peach

6. _____ spaghetti

7. _____ chilli

8. _____ cheese

Thinking Skills One

Food Expressions

People who work in a diner or restaurant sometimes use their own "slang" to describe each dish in a short way.

Example: **a hot dog** - a red bow-wow
jello - a nervous pudding

Think of your own slang for the following dishes:

1. Chocolate milkshake: _____

2. Hamburger:_____

3. Eggs on toast: _____

4. Tuna sandwich:_____

5. Strawberry jello: _____

6. Scrambled eggs: _____

7. Beef stew: _____

8. Butterscotch pudding: _____

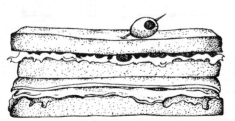

Thinking Skills Two

Riddles

Think about a food that you enjoy eating.

Make a riddle card about your food.

You will need to include **three** clues about:

- which food group it belongs to

- where it can be found/where it grows

- how it looks or tastes

Print the clues on the outside of your riddle card.

Draw a picture with your answer inside the card.

Example:

I am a fruit.
I grow in hot countries.
I have a greenish-yellow
shell and pale yellow flesh.

Riddle

I am a pineapple.

Answer

FOOD
Nutrition & Invention

Thinking Skills Three

A Food Career

Think of all the people who work each day to provide us with food.

List **six** careers that are involved in growing, processing or selling food.

1. _____

2. _____

3. _____

4. _____

5. _____

6. _____

Thinking Skills Four

Which Cereal Is That?

The breakfast cereal that we eat can be made of wheat, rice, corn or oats.

Can you think of **two** breakfast cereals for each type of grain?

List your answers in chart form.

Example:

wheat	rice
corn	oats

Thinking Skills Five

Advertisements

Think of all the advertisements for food that you have see on television, in magazines and on billboards, or heard on the radio.

Choose **one** of the advertisements and complete the following:

1. List the slogan or promise.

2. Explain what you think it means.

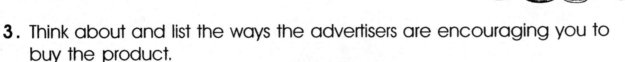

3. Think about and list the ways the advertisers are encouraging you to buy the product.

FOOD
Nutrition & Invention

Thinking Skills Six

Exercises for a Couch Potato

You have a friend who is a couch potato.

Think about the exercises he or she can do to get fit again.

Describe the actions he or she must do under each of these "Couch Potato" exercises.

Potato Peeler	Mashed Potato
Pota-toe Stretch	**Potato Chipper**

FOOD
Nutrition & Invention

Thinking Skills Seven

Invent a Wonder Food

Invent a **"wonder food"** that is very good for you.

You will need to think about:

• Will it be frozen or fresh?

• What ingredients will you use?

• How does it taste?

• What health-giving powers does it have?

• What will you call it?

Describe your "wonder food" and draw a picture to show how you will package

Research Activity One

Sugar Detective

Read the list of ingredients on the labels of canned or packaged foods or drinks.

Do the ingredients include sugar?

If the ingredients don't include sugar, see if the ingredients include:

- **sucrose**   - **fructose**   - **glucose**   - **maltose**   - **lactose**

These mean sugar too.

Make a list of sweet or savory foods or drinks that contain sugar.

Example:

Food	Sweet or Savory	Type of Sugar
hot dogs	savory	sugar

Research Activity Two

Traditions

At North American weddings there is usually a special cake for the bride and groom. It is called a Wedding Cake.

When a baby is born in China, its family paints some eggs red to give the baby good luck.

Research and find another tradition that involves food.

You will need to include:

- the name of the country it is from

- what kind of food is eaten or decorated

- a description of how this food is used and what it represents

Research Activity Three

Guess Who's Coming to Dinner?

Each day we eat foods from all over the world.

Research to find out which country the foods listed first came from.

Locate the country on a world map.

Label a blank map with the name of the country and the food that is produced there.

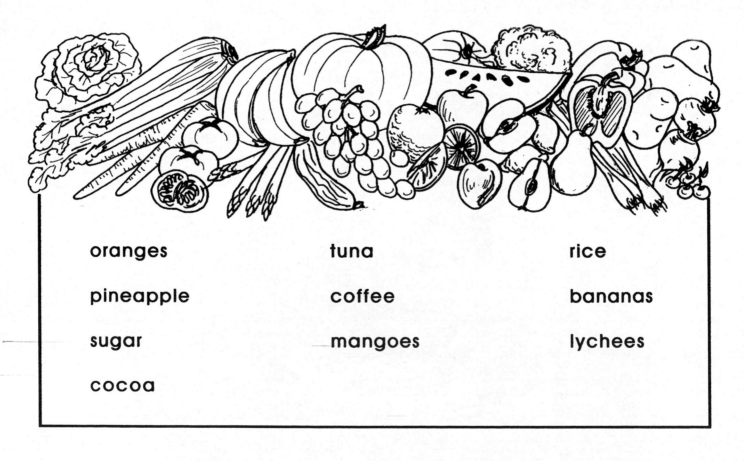

oranges	tuna	rice
pineapple	coffee	bananas
sugar	mangoes	lychees
cocoa		

Research Activity Four

Herbs

We use many different herbs in our cooking.

Research **one** of the following herbs.

You will need to include:

- a description and drawing of the plant

- a list of dishes this herb can be used in

oregano	thyme	basil
sage	chicory	mint
chives	caraway	anise
fennel	savory	cress

Research Activity Five

Introduced Foods

Many foods that we grow in North America were introduced from other countries.

Choose **one** of the following foods and research its history.

Describe how it came to North America.

potatoes	apples	tomatoes
wheat	oats	barley

Research Activity Six

Inventions

Food has been used for many things other than nutrition.

Example: | Corn has been used for fuel.

Research to find out how another food has been used for a new purpose.

Name the food and describe how it is used.

Research Activity Seven

Ethnic Foods

Many of the foods that we eat were brought here by people from all over the world.

Choose **one** of the countries below.

Research in an atlas to find out three facts about this country.

Trace a map of the country and label it.

List your **three** facts under the map.

China - rice	**Germany - hamburger**
Italy - pasta	**Mexico - tacos**

Creative Writing One

Alliteration

Make an A B C book all about food.

Use alliteration on each page to make it interesting.

Example: **Apples always appear appetizing.**

Blueberries bloom in bushes.

Illustrate each page of your book.

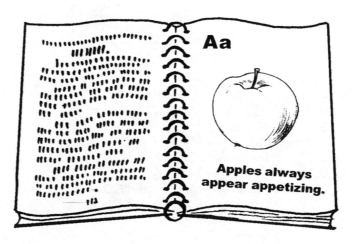

Creative Writing Two

Journal of an Explorer

Imagine that you are an explorer in search of spices or a tropical fruit.

Think about:

- which part of the world you will explore

- who will travel with you

- what problems you might experience and how you will solve them

- how you will bring back and use this spice or food

Describe your adventures as you search for your spice or fruit.

FOOD
Nutrition & Invention

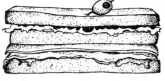

Creative Writing Three

Amazing Menu

You have just opened your own restaurant.

Create an amazing menu that will please your customers.

Include foods from all four food groups.

You will need to think about a theme for your restaurant. Will it be Seafood, 1950s Style, Health Food, Hot and Spicy or Barbecue?

Perhaps it will be a theme that you can think of yourself.

List your menu under the following headings.

Draw a picture of how the front of your restaurant will look.

How will the sign represent your theme?

Appetizers	Entrees	Desserts

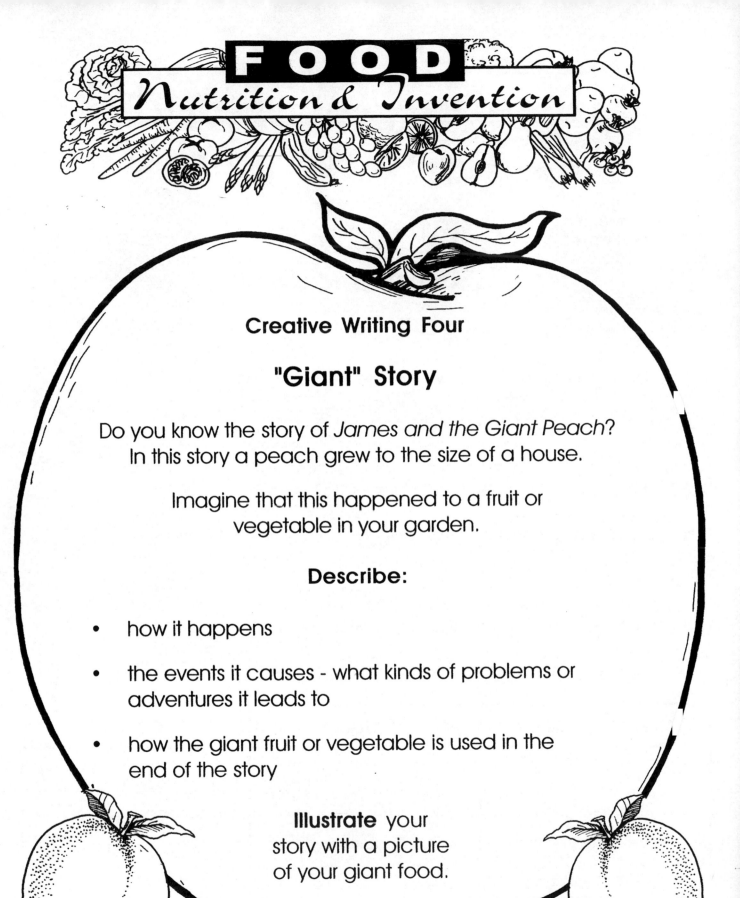

Creative Writing Four

"Giant" Story

Do you know the story of *James and the Giant Peach*? In this story a peach grew to the size of a house.

Imagine that this happened to a fruit or vegetable in your garden.

Describe:

- how it happens

- the events it causes - what kinds of problems or adventures it leads to

- how the giant fruit or vegetable is used in the end of the story

Illustrate your story with a picture of your giant food.

Creative Writing Five

Recipe Book

Look at some recipe books.

Choose **three** recipes that you would like to cook.

Copy the recipes in your best handwriting

Illustrate each recipe.

Make your recipes into a booklet.

Give your booklet a title.

Example:

"Recipes for
Chocolate Lovers"

Creative Writing Six

Illustrate a Poem

Look at some books with poems about food.

Choose a poem that you like.

Copy the poem on a blank piece of paper in your best handwriting.

Think about the pictures that you see in your mind when you read the poem.

Illustrate your poem with these pictures.

Creative Writing Seven

The "Hole" Story

Do you know how the doughnut was invented?

Make up your own story to explain how this happened.

You will need to describe:

- the characters involved

- the setting (where and when it happened)

- the problems the inventor experienced and how these were solved

- other people's reactions to the new invention - how did it become such a success?

Art Activity One

Design a "Super Plant"

The world needs a plant food that can survive any climate.

Design a plant that is resistant to drought, heat and cold.

This "super plant" will need a sturdy stalk.

Think about how your plant will look and taste.

1. Will it be a fruit, vegetable or grain?

2. How will it taste?

3. Will it have prickles?

4. How will the flowers and seeds look?

5. How big will it be?

6. What name will you give your plant?

Draw a picture of your "super plant" and label each part.

Art Activity Two

Pasta Bridge

Design a picture of what your bridge will look like before you begin.

You will need to think about:

- the height, width and length of your bridge (maximum length is 60 centimeters or 24 inches)

- which types of pasta you will use

- how you will support your bridge

Example:

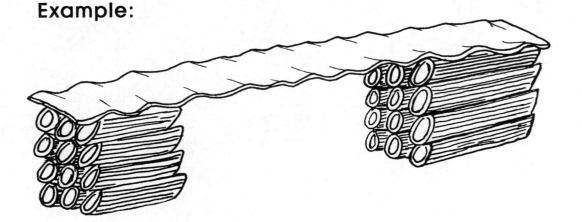

Art Activity Three

Cartoon Invention

Read in the Information Cards about how different foods, such as bubble gum, were invented.

In a cartoon, illustrate the steps the inventor went through.

You will need to create at least **three** frames for your cartoon.

Example:

FOOD
Nutrition & Invention

Art Activity Four

Snack Collage

Collect wrappers or advertisements of different snack foods.

Place them on a large piece of construction paper in an attractive design.

Glue each one in place to create a collage.

Give your collage a title.

Example:

Art Activity Five

Couch Potato Fitness

Create a poster or T-shirt design that will encourage couch potatoes to get up and exercise.

You will need to think about:

- a catchy title for you poster

- what type of exercise you will expect the couch potatoes to try

- how you will present this on your T-shirt or poster

Example:

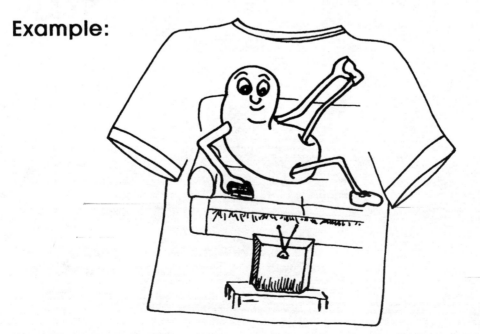

Answer Key
Student Booklet

Use this booklet to introduce new concepts and develop theme vocabulary. Complete one or two pages each day before students begin center activities or as an alternative to center time. Read through each cloze passage or activity with your students to ensure comprehension and as a springboard to further discussion.

Page One - You Are What You Eat: *(page 13)*
Discuss each of the four food groups and the appropriate number of servings for the age of the students. Have students record the foods that they ate during the previous day and the corresponding number of servings.

Page Two - Milk Products: *(page 14)*
You may wish to use an overhead to display the cloze passage or number the answers in order on the blackboard.
Answers are in the following order:

1. cows	4. germs	7. buttermilk	10. processed cheese
2. goats	5. pasteurized	8. rennet	11. taste
3. calcium	6. cream	9. whey	12. gelatin

Page Three - Meat and Alternatives: *(page 15)*
Answer to the cloze passage are as follows:

1. body building	4. beef	7. peanut butter	10. fish farms
2. vegetarian	5. poultry	8. free range	11. carp
3. eggs	6. fish	9. fishing	12. shellfish

Page Four - Grain Products: *(page 16)*
Answers are in the following order:

1. seeds	4. wheat	7. wheat germ	10. corn
2. cereals	5. flour	8. rice	11. corn meal
3. carbohydrates	6. bran	9. breakfast cereal	12. oat bran

Page Five - Vegetables: *(page 17)*
Answers to the passage are in the following order:

1. vitamins   2. sickness   3. energy   4. potato   5. leaves   6. roots   7. fruits

Brainstorm with your students vegetables belonging in each of the categories and have them record these in their booklet. Suggestions include:

Leaves: lettuce, cabbage, spinach, parsley
Flowers: broccoli, cauliflower
Seeds: corn, peas, beans
Stalks/Stems: celery, asparagus, rhubarb, sugar cane
Roots: carrots, parsnips, radishes
Tubers/Bulbs: white potatoes (tubers), onions (bulbs)

Page Six to Seven - Fruit *(page 18 - 19)*
Answers to the cloze passage are as follows:

1. vitamin C   2. pomes   3. drupes   4. berries   5. citrus
6. tropical   7. melon   8. bushes   9. trees

Brainstorm with your students further fruits that belong to each category. Have them record these in the chart. Suggestions include:

Pomes: apples, pears
Drupes: cherries, peaches, plums, apricots
Berries: strawberries, blueberries, grapes, cranberries
Citrus Fruits: oranges, lemons, grapefruit, kumquats
Tropical Fruits: bananas, pineapple, papaya, guava
Melons: watermelons, cantaloupes

Page Eight - The Food Chain: *(page 20)*
Explain to your students that a food chain is a chain of plants and animals that are linked together; an animal eats a plant and is in turn, eaten by a larger animal, etc. Have students draw and label each link in their own chain or use strips of construction paper, labeled, linked together to represent the food chain.

Page Nine to Ten - Your Sense of Taste: *(page 21 - 22)*

Answers in the following order are:

1. tongue	**2.** taste buds	**3.** sweet	**4.** salty
5. sour	**6.** bitter	**7.** smell	**8.** cold
9. water	**10.** saliva	**11.** throat	**12.** digest

Brainstorm with your students foods that belong to each of the "taste" categories and have them record these in their chart. Suggestions include:

Sweet: bananas, candy, cookies, sugar, molasses, honey
Salty: pretzels, potato chips, sauerkraut
Sour: lemons, limes
Bitter: unsweetened chocolate

Page Eleven to Twelve - Do You Have a Sweet Tooth? *(page 23 - 24)*

Answers to the cloze passage are as follows:

1. ketchup	**2.** breakfast cereals	**3.** sucrose	**4.** fructose
5. glucose	**6.** maltose	**7.** lactose	**8.** refined sugar
9. digest	**10.** energy	**11.** fruit	**12.** honey

Page Thirteen - Keeping Food Fresh: *(page 25)*

Use student input to create a chart listing processed foods under each heading. Suggestions include:

Vegetables and Fruits: canned, frozen, dried (beans, soup mixes)
Milk: canned, processed cheese, powdered/dried, pasteurized, yogurt
Fish: frozen, canned, dried, smoked (kippers), salted, pickled (herring)
Meat: canned, dried, smoked (ham, bacon), salted, processed (bolonga etc.) with preservatives

Page Fourteen - Food From Many Lands: *(page 26)*

Introduce this topic by brainstorming ethnic foods available within your community. You may wish to display some cookbooks focusing on foods from other countries, such as the Caribbean, Africa, South America, India and Mexico, as well as Europe. Discuss the term "staple food". Ask students to identify the staple food/s of their country. Answers to the menu quiz are as follows:

Menu 1: Country - Mexico	Staple Food - corn tortilla
Menu 2: Country - Norway	Staple Food - wheat bread
Menu 3: Country - Nigeria	Staple Food - yam and cassava
Menu 4: Country - India	Staple Food - chapatis and rice

Page Fifteen - In a Pickle: *(page 27)*

Brainstorm with your students expressions based on food. Record these on a chart or blackboard and have students choose one and illustrate its literal meaning. See the List of Vocabulary for suggestions.

Page Sixteen - Are You a Food Expert? *(page 28)*

Discuss the difference between fact and opinion. Answers to the quiz are as follows:

1. F	**2.** O	**3.** O	**4.** F	**5.** O	**6.** O	**7.** O	**8.** F

Activity Sheets

Reading Information Activity One: *(page 37)*

Part A

1. True	**2.** False	**3.** False	**4.** True

Part B

1. vanilla	**2.** New York City	**3.** home ice cream maker

Part C
Answers may vary.

Reading Information Activity Two: *(page 38)*

Part A
Answers may vary.

Part B

1. Roast Spanish peanuts	**2.** Let them cool	**3.** Take off the skins	**4.** Grind the peanuts up

Part C
1. protein, digest 2. sugar, salt
3. solid lump, oil

Reading Information Activity Three: (page 39)
Part A
Answers may vary.
Part B
1. George Crumb
2. because a customer asked him
3. Saratoga Chips
4. because they were made by hand
5. potato peeling machine

Reading Information Activity Four: (page 40)
Part A
1. Native People
2. resin from the black spruce tree
3. too sticky 4. Japan
Part B
Answers may vary.

Reading Information Activity Five: (page 41)
Part A
Answers may vary.
Part B
It makes your heart beat faster and when you first drink it, your body may feel like it is racing. Soon after you will feel tired. This happens because pop is made with caffeine and once your body uses up the caffeine you feel tired. There is no "real" food in pop for your body to use for energy, only sugar and water.
Part C
Answers may vary.

Reading Information Activity Six: (page 42)
Part A
1. digest 2. Kellogg's Toasted Corn Flakes
3. advertisements 4. sugar 5. meal
Part B
Answers may vary.

Reading Information Activity Seven: (page 43)
Part A, B, and C
Answers may vary.

Reading Information Activity Eight: (page 44)
Part A
1. ginger 2. cloves 3. cinnamon
4. nutmeg 5. pepper
Part B
1. cinnamon 2. nutmeg or ginger
Part C
1. cinnamon 2. nutmeg 3. cloves
Part D
1. pepper 2. chili
Part E
1. nutmeg 2. cinnamon or ginger

Language Activity One: (page 45)
1. In a saucepan, mix sugar, cornstarch, flour andsalt. Gradually add hot water, stirring constantly. Cook and stir over moderate heat till mixture comes to a boil. Reduce heat, cook and stir two minutes longer. Remove from heat.

2. Stir a moderate amount of hot mixture into egg yolks, then return to hot mixture. Bring mixture to boiling and cook two minutes, stirring constantly. Add butter and lemon peel slowly. Add lemon juice, mixing well.

3. Pour into pastry shell. Spread meringue over filling. Bake at 350°F for twelve to fifteen minutes. Cool before cutting.

Language Activity Two: (page 46)
1. pear/pair 2. whole/hole
3. meet/meat 4. piece/peace
5. stake/steak 6. bury/berry
7. plane/plain 8. beat/beet

Language Activity Three: (page 47)
1. calorie - a unit of the energy supplied by food
2. energy - capacity for doing work such as lifting or moving an object
3. vegetarian - a person who eats only vegetable foods and refrains from eating meat
4. nutrient - a nourishing substance, especially as an element or ingredient of a foodstuff
5. digestion - the digesting or breaking down of food
6. famine - the lack of food in a place, time of starving
7. protein - one of the substances containing nitrogen, carbon, hydrogen and oxygen that is a necessary part of the cells of animals and plants
8. fiber - a substance made from carbon dioxide and water by green plants in sunlight
10. vitamin - any one of certain special substances necessary for the normal growth and proper nourishment of the body

Language Activity Four: (page 48)
1. sour 2. cold 3. neat
4. dry 5. full
6. raw 7. frozen 8. worst
9. fresh 10. little

Language Activity Five and Six: (page 49 - 50)
Answers may vary.

Thinking Skills Activity Three: (page 53)
Answers may vary.
1. butcher 2. baker 3. farmer
4. manufacturer 5. harvester 6. grocer